EMPOWERING ARTISTRY

NAVIGATING THE LEGAL LANDSCAPE

KESÍA RAMOS

CONTENTS

PREFACE

Welcome to "Empowering Artistry: Navigating the Legal Landscape," a comprehensive manual designed to bridge the gap between artistic creativity and legal acumen. As a seasoned manager of a renowned artist and a business owner, I've witnessed firsthand the complexities and challenges artists face in safeguarding their legal rights. This manual is born from a decade of experience and a deep understanding of the artistic journey. Additionally, I've collaborated closely with an AI assistant in creating this guide, ensuring its richness, accuracy, and relevance for artists at any career stage.

Here, you'll find practical advice, real-life examples, and user-friendly guides tailored for artists at any career stage. My journey, marked by managing art projects, negotiating contracts, and balancing personal endeavors like homeschooling, has equipped me with unique insights I'm eager to share.

This manual is more than a legal guide; it's a tool to empower artists, fostering confidence in managing the legal dimensions of their craft. It combines my practical experience, industry knowledge, and a heartfelt desire to support the artistic community.

Join me on this journey to demystify legal jargon, navigate contracts, and protect your creative rights. After reading this manual, I aim to ensure that you'll be an artist and a legally savvy creator equipped to face the evolving art world confidently. Let's embark on this journey together, empowering your artistry every step of the way.

LEGAL DISCLAIMER

The information in "Empowering Artistry: Navigating the Legal Landscape" is only for general informational and educational purposes. The author of this manual is not a lawyer, and the content should not be considered legal advice.

While this manual aims to provide artists with a comprehensive overview of various aspects of contracts, negotiations, and artwork protection based on the author's experience in the industry, it is not intended to substitute for the advice of a professional legal advisor.

Readers are advised to consult with a qualified attorney on legal matters pertaining to their specific circumstances and to ensure compliance with their jurisdiction's current laws and regulations. The author makes no representations or warranties, express or implied, as to the accuracy, completeness, or suitability of the information contained in this manual.

Using the information in this manual, the reader agrees not to hold the author liable for any losses, injuries, or damages resulting from its display or use. All information is provided on an as-is basis.

- *Laws and regulations are subject to change; therefore, the information provided in this manual may reflect only some current legal developments.*

Welcome to Your Legal Empowerment

Welcome, artists and creators! You are about to embark on a transformative journey that bridges the vibrant world of art with the structured realm of law. This manual, "Empowering Artistry: Navigating the Legal Landscape," is crafted with a singular vision: to demystify the legalities that often seem like a foreign land to creative minds. Here, you'll find a sanctuary of knowledge where complex legal terms are translated into the language of art and where the seemingly impenetrable walls of contracts and agreements become navigable paths.

The Purpose of This Manual

Art is not just a manifestation of your creative spirit; it's also a testament to your professional identity. In the ever-evolving world of art, where your creations travel across diverse platforms and collaborations, understanding the legal aspects of your work is no longer a luxury—it's a necessity. This manual is designed to empower you with that understanding. It's tailored for you, the artist, whether you're taking your first steps in the professional world or are a seasoned creator seeking to reinforce your legal knowledge.

What You Will Discover:

- <u>Demystifying Legal Jargon</u>: Unravel the complex language of law, making it accessible and understandable.

- <u>Contract Anatomy</u>: Learn what each clause means for you and your art by diving deep into the structure of contracts.

- <u>Navigating NDAs</u>: Master the intricacies of Non-Disclosure Agreements, ensuring your ideas stay protected.

- <u>Negotiation Strategies</u>: Develop skills to negotiate contracts that respect your art and your rights.

- <u>Avoiding Pitfalls</u>: Learn to identify and avoid common legal pitfalls in the art world.

- <u>Protecting Your Rights</u>: Gain knowledge on safeguarding your most valuable asset—your intellectual property.

Our Approach

This manual is more than just a compilation of guidance on legal considerations for artists; it's a journey tailored for the artistic soul. The language is clear, the examples are relevant, and the direction is practical. Each chapter builds upon the last, forming a comprehensive guide that grows with your understanding. And at the heart of it all is a message of empowerment: with knowledge comes power—the power to protect your work, to stand up for your rights, and to navigate the art world with confidence and peace of mind.

Your Invincible Tool

As you turn these pages, envision them as tools in your artistic arsenal, equipping you to face the legal dimensions of your craft with confidence and savvy. Remember, understanding your art's legalities protects your work and honors your identity as an artist.

Empowering Your Contract Negotiations

As you navigate the legal aspects of your artistic career, remember that contracts, often perceived as daunting, are the gateways to your rights and opportunities. It's essential to understand that everything within a contract is negotiable. This manual aims to demystify legal jargon and empower you to approach contracts with a negotiator's mindset. Doing so allows you to tailor agreements to suit your needs better and protect your interests.

Welcome to a journey of empowerment.

1

UNDERSTANDING BASIC LEGAL TERMS

Deciphering the Language of Law in Art

A
s an artist, stepping into the legal aspects of your career can feel like navigating uncharted waters. The key to confident navigation? Understanding the language. In this chapter, "Deciphering the Language of Law in Art," we'll transform legal jargon into clear, understandable terms, illuminating the path for your artistic endeavors.

Copyright: Your Artistic Shield

- Definition: The exclusive legal right, given to you as the creator, to publish, reproduce, distribute, display, license, and sell your original work.
- In Practice: Imagine you create a painting. Copyright lets you decide who can make, display, or sell copies.
- Why It Matters: It protects your work from being used without your permission, ensuring you get the credit and compensation you deserve.

- *For example, Only the copyright holder can legally authorize copies or adaptations of their work.*

Licensing: Sharing Your Work on Your Terms

- <u>Definition</u>: Permission that you, as the copyright holder, give to someone else to use your work under specific conditions.
- <u>In Practice</u>: If a company wants to use your artwork for its ads, a license agreement dictates how they can use it and what you get in return.
- <u>Why It Matters</u>: Licensing lets you profit from your work while controlling its use.

Intellectual Property: The Realm of Creative Rights

- <u>Definition</u>: Legal rights arising from intellectual activity in the industrial, scientific, literary, and artistic fields.
- <u>In Practice</u>: Your unique artistic style, method, or concept is your intellectual property.
- <u>Why It Matters</u>: It's the legal recognition of your creativity, giving you ownership and rights over your unique creations.

Work-for-Hire: Understanding Creative Ownership

- <u>Definition</u>: A work created by an employee as part of their job or a work specially ordered or commissioned for certain types of use, where the employer or the person who commissioned the work is considered the legal author.
- <u>In Practice:</u> For instance, if a company commissions you to create a piece of artwork, the work-for-hire agreement

may state that the company owns the artwork, not you as the artist.

- <u>Why It Matters:</u> Understanding work-for-hire is crucial for artists because it can significantly impact who holds the copyright and control over the artwork. It determines whether you retain ownership of your creations or if they belong to the employer or commissioner.

Indemnification: Your Financial Safety Net

- <u>Definition</u>: A contractual agreement to compensate for any losses or damages incurred.
- <u>In Practice</u>: Indemnification can protect you financially if someone sues you for copyright infringement in a work you sold.
- <u>Why It Matters:</u> It's a safety measure that ensures you're not financially responsible for unexpected legal issues related to your work.

Jurisdiction: Setting the Legal Stage

- <u>Definition</u>: The authority given to legal bodies over some geographic regions and types of legal cases.
- <u>In Practice</u>: If you sign a contract in the U.S., but your buyer is in France, jurisdiction determines which country's laws apply if there's a dispute.
- <u>Why It Matters:</u> It influences how legal issues are resolved and what laws protect your work.

Royalties: Earning from Your Creations

- Definition: Payments made to rights holders (such as artists or composers) for using or selling their work, typically a percentage of revenue.
- In Practice: If your artwork is reproduced as prints or used in advertising, you receive a percentage of the sales or usage fees as royalties.
- Why It Matters: Understanding and negotiating royalties is crucial for artists who license their work, as it directly impacts how you earn ongoing income and retain economic ties to your creations.

Confidentiality Agreement: Securing Sensitive Information

- Definition: A legal agreement between parties to not disclose information covered by the contract. It is often a component of NDAs.
- In Practice: When discussing a potential collaboration or project with a gallery, a confidentiality agreement ensures that any shared ideas, strategies, or designs remain private.
- Why It Matters: These agreements are essential in negotiations with galleries, agents, and clients to protect sensitive information about your art projects or business practices, safeguarding your competitive edge.

Assignment Clause: Transferring Rights and Responsibilities

- Definition: A clause in a contract that allows one party to transfer its rights and obligations under the agreement to another party.
- In Practice: If you sign a contract to create a mural, an assignment clause could allow the contracting party to

transfer the agreement to another entity, changing who
you are legally obligated to.
- <u>Why It Matters</u>: Artists should be aware of contract
  assignment clauses, as they can impact who controls the
  rights to your work and with whom you're ultimately
  working.

Termination Clause: Understanding Contract Endings

- <u>Definition</u>: A provision in a contract that outlines the
  conditions under which the contract can be ended before
  the completion of its term.
- <u>In Practice</u>: If unforeseen circumstances arise, a
  termination clause can outline the conditions under
  which either you or the client can end the contract, such
  as failure to meet deadlines or payment issues.
- <u>Why It Matters</u>: Helps artists understand under what
  circumstances a contract can be terminated, protecting
  them from abrupt or unjustified contract endings and
  providing a clear exit strategy.

Force Majeure: Protection from Unforeseen Events

- <u>Definition</u>: A contract clause frees both parties from
  liability or obligation when an extraordinary event or
  circumstance beyond their control prevents one or both
  parties from fulfilling their duties.
- <u>In Practice</u>: If a natural disaster prevents you from
  completing a commissioned sculpture on time, a force
  majeure clause could protect you from legal and financial
  penalties.
- <u>Why It Matters</u>: This clause protects artists in case of
  unforeseeable events like natural disasters, war, or

pandemics, ensuring they are not held liable for situations beyond their control.

End-of-Chapter Summary:

Understanding these legal terms is like having a compass in art law. It empowers you to make informed decisions, protect your work, and confidently engage in professional relationships. Armed with this knowledge, you're not just an artist; you're an informed creator with the power to navigate the legalities of your artistic journey.

~

Real-Life Scenario - Applying Legal Terms

Scenario Title: The Cross-Country Art Exhibition

- **Background:** You are a visual artist invited to participate in a prestigious art exhibition in a different country. For three months, the exhibition organizers want to feature one of your most famous works, "The Colors of Life," in their main gallery. They have sent you a contract to formalize the arrangement.
- **Task:** Review the hypothetical contract provided and identify how the legal terms from Chapter 1 apply in this context. Consider the implications of each term for your rights and responsibilities as an artist.

Hypothetical Contract Excerpts:

1. COPYRIGHT CLAUSE: "THE ARTIST RETAINS FULL COPYRIGHT OF 'THE COLORS OF LIFE.' THE EXHIBITION ORGANIZERS ARE GRANTED TEMPORARY RIGHTS TO DISPLAY THE ARTWORK FOR THE EXHIBITION'S DURATION."

2. LICENSING AGREEMENT: "THE ARTIST GRANTS THE ORGANIZERS NON-EXCLUSIVE RIGHTS TO USE IMAGES OF 'THE COLORS OF LIFE' FOR PROMOTIONAL PURPOSES RELATED TO THE EXHIBITION."

3. JURISDICTION: "ANY DISPUTES ARISING FROM THIS AGREEMENT SHALL BE SETTLED UNDER THE LAWS OF THE COUNTRY WHERE THE EXHIBITION IS HELD."

4. INDEMNIFICATION CLAUSE: "THE ARTIST AGREES TO INDEMNIFY THE ORGANIZERS AGAINST ANY CLAIMS OF COPYRIGHT INFRINGEMENT RELATED TO 'THE COLORS OF LIFE.'"

5. FORCE MAJEURE: "NEITHER PARTY SHALL BE LIABLE FOR FAILURE TO PERFORM ITS OBLIGATIONS IF SUCH FAILURE IS DUE TO EVENTS BEYOND ITS REASONABLE CONTROL, SUCH AS NATURAL DISASTERS OR POLITICAL UNREST."

Real-Life Scenario - Questions

Questions for Consideration:

- How does the copyright clause protect your interests as an artist?
- What are the limitations and benefits of the licensing agreement for you and the organizers?
- Why is it important to understand the jurisdiction clause in this international context?
- How might the indemnification clause impact you, and what precautions should you take?
- In what situations would the force majeure clause be relevant, and how does it protect both parties?

Reflection:

- Reflect on the importance of understanding these legal terms and their practical implications.
- Consider how being well-informed about legal aspects can influence your decisions and agreements in international collaborations.

Chapter 1 Quiz: Understanding Basic Legal Terms

1. What does 'Copyright' give an artist the power to control?

A) Where the art is displayed

B) Who can make copies or sell the art

C) The price of the art

D) The colors used in the art

2. What is a 'Confidentiality Agreement' often a component of?

A) NDAs

B) Royalty agreements

C) Assignment clauses

D) Force Majeure clauses

3. In a 'Work-for-Hire' agreement, who is generally considered the legal author?

A) The artist

B) The employer or commissioner

C) The public

D) The Gallery

4. What does 'Jurisdiction' determine in a legal dispute?

A) The compensation amounts

B) Which country's laws apply

C) The artwork's value

D) The length of the trial

5. What is the primary purpose of a 'Force Majeure' clause in a contract?

A) To set payment terms

B) To protect parties in case of unforeseen events

C) To define the artwork's scope

D) To assign copyright

Answer Key:

1. B) Who can make copies or sell the art

2. A) NDAs

3. B) The employer or commissioner

4. B) Which country's laws apply

5. B) To protect parties in case of unforeseen events

2

ANATOMY OF A CONTRACT

Navigating the Blueprint of Art Contracts

I n the art world, contracts are the blueprints of professional relationships. They outline the expectations, roles, and responsibilities of each party. This chapter, "Navigating the Blueprint of Art Contracts," guides you through the anatomy of a typical art contract, ensuring you understand each part and its significance to your artistic endeavors.

Project Overview: Setting the Stage

- Explanation: This section defines the project's scope, including the nature of the work to be created and its purpose.
- In Practice: For example, a commission for a mural would detail its size, location, and theme.
- Key Considerations: Ensure the project's scope aligns with your creative vision and capabilities.

Scope of Work: The Nitty-Gritty Details

- Explanation: Outlines materials, project phases, and collaboration requirements.
- In Practice: If you're painting a mural, this would include the type of paint, preparation work, and any assistance you might need.
- Key Considerations: Look for clarity in this section to avoid future disputes about expectations.

Timeline: Mapping Out the Journey

- Explanation: Sets out the timeline for the project, including start and completion dates and any key milestones.
- In Practice: A timeline for a mural might include dates for initial sketches, the start of painting, and the expected completion.
- Key Considerations: Ensure the timeline is realistic and provides enough flexibility for the artistic process and potential delays.

Payment Terms: The Art of Compensation

- Explanation: Details of how and when you will be paid, including any advance payments, installments, and the final payment.
- In Practice: This could include a down payment before work begins, followed by payments at specified milestones.
- Key Considerations: Look for fairness in payment terms and ensure they align with your cash flow needs.

Intellectual Property and Copyright: Protecting Your Creations

- <u>Explanation</u>: Specifies who owns the intellectual property rights to the artwork.
- <u>In Practice</u>: This might include rights for reproducing or using artwork in promotional materials.
- <u>Key Considerations</u>: Clarify ownership rights to ensure your work is protected and used as agreed.

Digital Art Contracts

- <u>Explanation</u>: Focus on digital reproduction, distribution, and usage rights.
- <u>In Practice</u>: Addressing scenarios like online sales, digital exhibitions, or the use of art in digital media.
- <u>Key Considerations</u>: Clarify the extent of digital rights granted and restrictions on digital reproduction.

Performance Art Agreements

- <u>Explanation</u>: Emphasize terms related to live performance details, artist safety, and audience engagement.
- <u>In Practice</u>: Contracts for performances in galleries, public spaces, or private events.
- <u>Key Considerations</u>: Specify performance conditions, safety measures, and audience interaction guidelines.

Case Study: Performance Art – Contractual Disputes and Artist Safety

- *Background: A performance artist signed a contract with a gallery for a live performance piece. During the performance, the artist was injured due to the gallery's negligence.*
- *Legal Focus: Contractual obligations regarding artist safety and liability.*

- *Outcome: The artist successfully sued the gallery for breach of contract and negligence.*

Installation Art Contracts

- <u>Explanation</u>: Outline agreements covering space usage, installation logistics, and maintenance responsibilities.
- <u>In Practice</u>: Contracts for installing artwork in galleries, public spaces, or art fairs.
- <u>Key Considerations</u>: Detail installation and de-installation responsibilities, display duration, and artwork insurance.

Traditional Art Mediums

- <u>Explanation</u>: Cover sale and exhibition of physical artworks, including reproduction rights and gallery representation.
- <u>In Practice</u>: Contracts for selling paintings or sculptures, gallery exhibitions, or art commissions.
- <u>Key Considerations</u>: Clearly define terms of sale, transport, insurance, and exhibition conditions.

Cross-Medium Collaboration Contracts

- <u>Explanation</u>: Address collaborative projects involving multiple art forms and artists.
- <u>In Practice</u>: Joint ventures like collaborative installations or multimedia exhibitions.
- <u>Key Considerations</u>: Establish clear roles, contribution expectations, and profit-sharing arrangements among all artists.

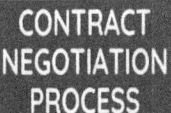

CONTRACT NEGOTIATION PROCESS

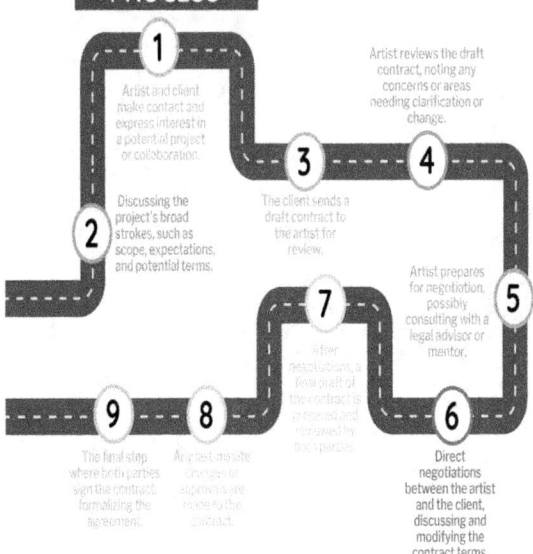

1 Artist and client make contact and express interest in a potential project or collaboration.

2 Discussing the project's broad strokes, such as scope, expectations, and potential terms.

3 The client sends a draft contract to the artist for review.

4 Artist reviews the draft contract, noting any concerns or areas needing clarification or change.

5 Artist prepares for negotiation, possibly consulting with a legal advisor or mentor.

6 Direct negotiations between the artist and the client, discussing and modifying the contract terms.

7 After negotiations, a final draft of the contract is prepared and reviewed by both parties.

8 Any last-minute changes or expenses are made to the contract.

9 The final step where both parties sign the contract, formalizing the agreement.

10 ART CONTRACT
Components

01.
Parties Involved

Identifying the artist and the client or any other parties involved in the contract.

A brief description of the project, including the type of artwork and its purpose.

02.
Project Overview

03.
Scope of Work

Detailed information about what is expected in the project, including the size, materials, and any specific requirements.

Outlining key dates, such as start and completion dates, and any milestones or deadlines.

04.
Timeline

05.
Payment Terms

Details about compensation, including total amount, payment schedule, and method of payment.

Clarification on who holds the copyright and any rights being licensed or transferred.

06.
Intellectual Property Rights

07.
Licensing Terms

If applicable, terms regarding the rights granted to the client for using the artwork.

Conditions under which the contract can be terminated by either party.

08.
Termination Clauses

09.
Dispute Resolution

Guidelines on how disputes related to the contract will be resolved.

The legal jurisdiction and the governing law under which the contract is enforceable.

10.
Jurisdiction & Governing Law

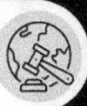

~

Understanding Non-Compete Clauses

Definition and Common Terms:

Non-compete clauses are contractual agreements restricting an individual's ability to engage in similar employment or projects within a specific geographic area and for a certain period after leaving or completing a project. These clauses protect a business's interests by preventing direct competition or sharing sensitive information with competitors.

Implications for Artists:

- **Career Limitations:** Non-compete clauses can significantly limit an artist's freedom to take on new projects or opportunities, particularly in the same industry or art form.
- **Duration and Scope:** Pay close attention to the time of the non-compete (how long it lasts) and its geographic scope (where it applies).
- **Specificity:** Vague or overly broad non-compete clauses can be more challenging. Clauses should be clear and specific to be enforceable.

Legality:

- The enforceability of non-compete clauses varies by jurisdiction. In some places, they are heavily regulated or not enforceable, especially if deemed unreasonable in scope, duration, or geographic limitation.

- It's crucial to understand the legal standards in your region.

Negotiation Strategies:

- **Seek Clarification and Limitations:** If presented with a non-compete clause, seek clarification on its terms and consider negotiating its scope, duration, and geographic limitations to be more favorable.
- **Legal Review:** Consult with a legal professional to understand the implications fully and to negotiate or possibly avoid the clause.
- **Alternative Arrangements:** Sometimes, it may be possible to agree on alternative arrangements, such as non-disclosure agreements, to protect the employer's interests without overly restricting your future opportunities.

Key Considerations When Presented With a Non-Compete Clause:

When presented with a non-compete clause in a contract, it's crucial to approach it thoughtfully. Here are some reflective questions to help you analyze the situation and make an informed decision:

1. Project Worth vs. Future Opportunities:

- **Is this project worth limiting my future project possibilities?** Consider the significance of the current project against the potential opportunities you might have to forgo.

2. Financial Compensation:

- **Does the project budget warrant such a restrictive ask?** Evaluate if the financial compensation for the project justifies the limitations imposed by the non-compete clause.

3. Long-Term Career Impact:

- **Am I open to declining new projects because of this one?** Reflect on how this agreement might affect your long-term career trajectory and opportunities.

4. Duration and Scope of the Clause:

- **How long and over what geographic area does the clause restrict me?** Assess whether the course and scope of the clause are reasonable and align with your career goals.

5. Alternative Opportunities:

- **Are there other opportunities available that do not require such restrictions?** Consider if declining the current offer might open doors to other projects without these limitations.

6. Negotiation Possibilities:

- **Can I negotiate the terms of the clause to be more favorable?** Consider aspects of the clause that can be modified to better suit your needs and career plans.

7. Legal Advice:

- **Should I consult a legal professional for advice on this clause?** If you need more clarification about the implications, seeking legal counsel can provide that.

~

Navigating Maintenance Clauses in Art Contracts

Understanding Maintenance Clauses: Maintenance clauses in art contracts specify who is responsible for the upkeep of the artwork after installation. These clauses are particularly relevant for paintings such as sculptures, installations, or murals, which may require ongoing maintenance to preserve their condition and appearance.

Key Elements of Maintenance Clauses:

- **Responsibility for Maintenance:** Clearly define who is responsible for the maintenance of the artwork. Typically, the artwork's client or owner bears this responsibility after installation or sale.
- **Scope of Maintenance:** Detail what maintenance is required, including cleaning, repairs, or protective measures.
- **Cost of Maintenance:** Establish who will bear the costs associated with maintenance. In most cases, this should be the client or the current owner of the artwork.
- **Timeframe for Maintenance:** Include guidelines on how often maintenance should be performed to ensure the artwork's longevity and integrity.

Why Maintenance Clauses Matter:

- **Protecting the Artwork:** Proper maintenance ensures the artwork remains in good condition and accurate to the artist's original vision.
- **Limiting Artist's Liability:** By specifying that the client is responsible for maintenance, the artist is not indefinitely

bound to care for the work, which can be time-consuming and costly.

- **Clear Expectations:** Clear maintenance terms prevent misunderstandings and potential disputes about the artwork's care.

Negotiating Maintenance Clauses:

- **Be Specific:** Ensure the maintenance clause is specific and unambiguous to avoid future disputes.
- **Consider the Artwork's Nature:** Tailor the maintenance clause based on the nature and needs of the artwork.
- **Seek Legal Advice:** If necessary, consult with a legal professional to draft a maintenance clause that adequately protects your interests and the artwork.

In Practice: For example, if you create a large outdoor sculpture, the maintenance clause in your contract might state that the client is responsible for regular cleaning and any necessary repairs, and this should occur at least once every two years at the client's expense.

Responsibility for Maintenance and Artist Compensation:

When the responsibility for maintenance falls on the artist, it's crucial to establish clear terms regarding compensation and additional expenses. This ensures that the artist is fairly reimbursed for their time and effort in maintaining the artwork.

1. **Separate Maintenance Fee:** If you, as the artist, are responsible for the maintenance of the artwork, ensure that this is not included in the original payment for creating the artwork. Maintenance should be compensated separately.

2. Budgeting for Maintenance: Negotiate a maintenance budget that covers:

- **Time and Labor:** Compensation for the time spent on maintaining the artwork.
- **Travel Expenses:** If the artwork is located away from your base, include travel expenses in the maintenance budget.
- **Accommodation and Living Expenses:** Ensure that accommodation and living expenses are covered for maintenance work requiring overnight stays.

3. Maintenance Contract: Consider drafting a separate maintenance contract or addendum to the original contract, which details:

- **Maintenance Services:** Specific tasks and frequency of maintenance work.
- **Duration of Responsibility:** Define how long you are expected to provide maintenance services.
- **Payment Terms:** Outline how and when you will be paid for maintenance work, including provisions for cost adjustments over time.

4. Maintenance Schedule and Agreement: Agree on a maintenance schedule that is practical and feasible for you. Ensure both parties agree on routine maintenance versus more significant repair or restoration work.

5. Legal and Contractual Advice: Seek legal advice to draft a maintenance clause or contract that protects your interests, especially if the maintenance obligations are extensive or complex.

In Practice: For instance, if you agree to maintain a mural you painted in a different city, the contract should stipulate a separate fee for each maintenance visit, including costs for travel, accommodation, and any necessary supplies, in addition to your labor fee.

Understanding and Negotiating Disclosure Statements

What is a Disclosure Statement? A disclosure statement in an art contract is a declaration by the artist about the artwork's condition, history, materials used, and any other relevant information. It provides the buyer or commissioner with essential facts about the artwork, thereby preventing future disputes or misunderstandings.

Key Elements of a Disclosure Statement:

- **Artwork Details:** Information about the medium, materials, techniques, and any unique artwork features.
- **Condition:** The current state of the artwork, including any imperfections or restoration work.
- **Provenance and Authenticity:** The artwork's history, previous ownership (if applicable), and any documentation verifying its authenticity.
- **Care Instructions:** Guidelines on how to care for and maintain the artwork.

Importance of Disclosure Statements:

- **Transparency:** Ensures the buyer is fully informed about their purchase.
- **Protecting the Artist:** Helps prevent future legal claims by disclosing all necessary information upfront.
- **Building Trust:** Establishes a foundation of trust and credibility with buyers and collectors.

Negotiating Disclosure Statements:

- **Be Comprehensive:** Include all relevant information about the artwork. Omitting details can lead to potential legal issues.
- **Clarity:** Ensure that the statement is clear and understandable to non-art professionals.
- **Legal Review:** If the artwork is high in value or the contract is complex, consider having a legal professional review the disclosure statement.

In Practice: For example, if you sell a sculpture, the disclosure statement should include the materials used, any special care needed to maintain its condition, and whether the sculpture has undergone any repairs.

Managing Revision Policies and Artwork Acceptance

Revision Policies:

- **Limit on Revisions:** It's practical to set a maximum number of revisions included in the initial contract price. A common approach is to allow up to three revisions.
- **Additional Revisions:** Clearly state that revisions beyond the agreed number will incur additional fees. For instance, you might charge $500 per additional revision. The exact amount can be set at your discretion based on the nature of the work and your standard rates.
- **Clear Definitions:** Define what constitutes a 'revision' in your contract. Distinguish between minor adjustments and significant changes that would be considered new revisions.

Example Clause: *The client is entitled to up to three artwork revisions at no additional cost. Any further modifications the client requests will be charged at $500 per revision.*

Artwork Acceptance Timeframes:

- **Clear Deadlines:** Establish a clear timeframe within which the client must review and accept the final artwork. A typical timeframe is seven business days from the delivery of the final artwork or mockup.
- **Non-Response Equals Acceptance:** Specify in the contract that if you do not receive any feedback or requests for changes within this timeframe, the artwork will be considered accepted by the client.
- **Communication:** Encourage open and timely communication with the client during the review period to address any concerns or required changes.

Example Clause: *Upon delivery of the final artwork, the client will have seven business days to review it and request changes. If no modification request is received within this timeframe, the client will deem the artwork accepted.*

Note on Contract Flexibility and Adaptation:

As you navigate the world of art contracts, it's important to recognize the value of flexibility and adaptation. While this chapter provides a framework for understanding standard clauses and contract structures, remember that every artistic engagement is unique. The nuances of each project, the specific demands of your art form, and the parties' individual needs can all influence the shape of a contract.

Adapting to Unique Situations:

- **Contextual Variations:** Be prepared to encounter contracts that deviate from standard templates. Each project might require bespoke clauses that reflect its specific circumstances.
- **Negotiation is Key:** Don't hesitate to negotiate terms that better align with your artistic goals and the project's unique aspects. Effective negotiation can lead to more favorable terms and a contract supporting your artistic vision and professional needs.

Embracing Contractual Diversity:

- **Learning Opportunity:** Each contract you encounter is an opportunity to learn and refine your understanding of legal agreements in the art world.
- **Seek Advice When Needed:** If you need clarification on a contract's terms or how to adapt them to your situation, consider consulting with a legal professional. Tailored advice can be invaluable in complex or high-stakes cases.

By embracing flexibility and adaptability in contract negotiations, you empower yourself to forge agreements that protect your rights and foster positive and productive professional relationships.

End-of-Chapter Summary:

Understanding each component of an art contract empowers you to negotiate and agree to terms that respect your art and your rights. It's about finding harmony between your artistic vision and the practicalities of a professional engagement. With this knowledge, you are better equipped to navigate contractual relationships confidently and clearly.

~

Sample Contract for Contract Analysis Exercise

Exercise Instructions:

<u>**Review the sample contract below and identify the following:**</u>

1. Critical sections and their purposes.
2. Any clauses that might need clarification or negotiation.
3. The rights and responsibilities of both the Artist and the Client.
4. Considerations regarding payment, timeline, and intellectual property.

ARTWORK COMMISSION AGREEMENT
 This Agreement is made on [Date] between:

- **Artist:** [Artist's Full Name], residing at [Artist's Address]
- **Client:** [Client's Full Name or Company Name], residing at [Client's Address]

1. Project Overview: The Artist agrees to create a [Description of Artwork], hereafter referred to as "the Artwork," for the Client.

2. Scope of Work:

- The Artwork will be a [specific description of the artwork, including size, materials, theme, etc.].
- The Artist will provide preliminary sketches for the Client's approval before proceeding to the final piece.

3. Timeline:

- Preliminary Sketches Due: [Date]
- Completion of Artwork: [Date]

4. Payment Terms:

- Total Commission Price: [Total Amount]
- Initial Deposit (50%): [Amount], due upon signing this agreement.
- Final Payment (50%): [Amount], due upon completion of the Artwork and before delivery.

5. Intellectual Property Rights:

- The Artist retains all copyright in the Artwork. The Client is granted a license to display the Artwork but may not reproduce it.
- The Artist has the right to use images of the Artwork for promotional purposes.

6. Confidentiality: Both parties agree to keep the details of this agreement and the artwork confidential until the agreed-upon public reveal date.

7. Cancellation and Termination:

- Either party may cancel this agreement with written notice. The Client will be responsible for payment of all work completed up to the point of cancellation.
- In case of cancellation, the initial deposit is non-refundable.

8. Force Majeure: Neither party shall be liable for failure to perform its obligations if such loss is due to events beyond its reasonable control, including but not limited to natural disasters and war.

IN WITNESS WHEREOF, the parties have executed this Agreement as of the date first written above.

Artist's
    Signature:_____
    Date: _____

Client's
    Signature: _____
    Date: _____

NAVIGATING NON-DISCLOSURE AGREEMENTS

Unveiling the Secrets of NDAs

Non-disclosure agreements (NDAs) can seem like a veil of secrecy over exciting opportunities. However, they are vital in protecting both your ideas and your collaborators. In "Unveiling the Secrets of NDAs," we'll decode what NDAs mean for you as an artist, helping you understand when and how to use them effectively.

1. Definition and Purpose of NDAs

- Explanation: Understand what NDAs are and why they are used in the art world.
- In Practice: For instance, when working on a collaborative project with a brand, an NDA ensures that the project details remain confidential until its public release.
- Key Considerations: Know when an NDA is necessary and what it should protect.

2. Key Clauses in NDAs

- Explanation: Break down the typical clauses found in NDAs and what they mean.
- In Practice: Clauses such as the definition of confidential information, the obligations of the receiving party, and the terms of the agreement.
- Key Considerations: Ensure the clauses are fair and do not overly restrict your artistic freedom or future opportunities.

3. Negotiating NDAs

- Explanation: Tips for negotiating NDAs that protect your interests without hindering your creative collaboration.
- In Practice: Strategies for discussing terms that seem overly restrictive or vague.
- Key Considerations: Balance the need for confidentiality with your own rights and career prospects.

Case Study: The International Art Collaboration

- Content: In 2018, a renowned artist based in New York collaborated with a tech company in Japan to create an interactive digital art installation. An NDA was signed to protect the innovative technology and creative concepts involved. However, the artist shared some details with a potential sponsor, violating the NDA. The tech company initiated legal action, resulting in a settlement that included financial compensation and public retraction. This case underscores the importance of respecting NDA terms and being aware of cultural differences in business practices.

- How could the artist better manage communication with external parties under an NDA?
- What steps could have been taken to prevent the breach of the NDA?

4. Common Misunderstandings and Pitfalls

- Explanation: Clarify common misconceptions and potential pitfalls in NDAs.
- In Practice: Misunderstanding the scope of confidentiality can lead to unintentional breaches of the agreement.
- Key Considerations: Clearly understand and comply with the terms and know the consequences of breaches.

Global Perspective on NDAs

Non-disclosure agreements can vary significantly across countries, influenced by local legal systems and cultural business practices. For example, European countries may have stricter privacy laws that impact NDA terms, while Asian business practices might emphasize relational agreements alongside formal NDAs. When engaging in international collaborations, it's crucial to understand these nuances. Consulting with legal professionals experienced in international law is advisable to ensure that the NDA respects global practices and legal requirements.

KEY TAKEAWAY: For artists working internationally, it's essential to recognize that the interpretation and enforceability of NDAs can differ globally. Awareness and professional guidance are vital to navigating these differences effectively.

Diagram for NDA Relationships

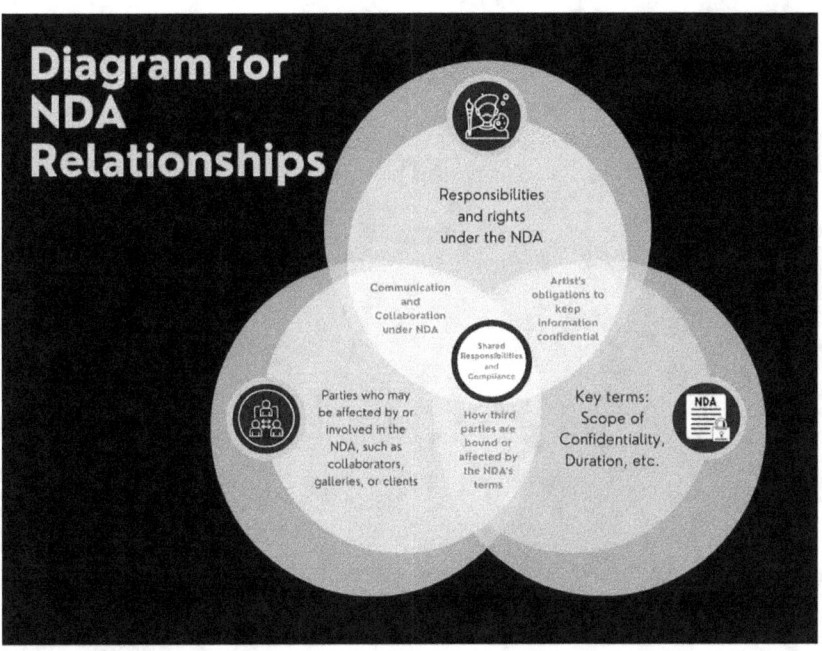

Responsibilities and rights under the NDA

Communication and Collaboration under NDA

Artist's obligations to keep information confidential

Shared Responsibilities and Compliance

Parties who may be affected by or involved in the NDA, such as collaborators, galleries, or clients

How third parties are bound or affected by the NDA's terms

Key terms: Scope of Confidentiality, Duration, etc.

Legal Repercussions of Breaking an NDA

Consequences of Breach:

Breaching an NDA can lead to significant legal and financial consequences. Depending on the nature of the breach and the sensitivity of the disclosed information, repercussions can include:

- <u>Lawsuits</u>: The party who issued the NDA may sue for breach of contract.
- <u>Financial Damages</u>: You could be liable for monetary damages, including compensating for any losses caused by the breach.
- <u>Criminal Charges</u>: In rare cases, especially where highly sensitive or proprietary information is involved, criminal charges could be filed.

Real-World Examples:

- **Case Study 1**: In the art world, a famous artist once faced a lawsuit for disclosing confidential details about a high-profile project they were involved in, which was covered under an NDA. The breach resulted in a substantial financial settlement.
- **Case Study 2**: A former tech company employee leaked trade secrets to a competitor in another industry, violating their NDA. The company pursued legal action, leading to severe financial penalties and criminal charges against the individual.

Key Considerations:

- <u>Understanding the Stakes</u>: Before signing, it's crucial to fully comprehend the terms of the NDA. Recognize the seriousness of these agreements and the potential impact of any breach.

- <u>Implications for Future Opportunities</u>: Consider how a breach could affect your reputation and future collaborations. Trust and professionalism are paramount in the art world, and breaching confidentiality can significantly damage your credibility.

Seeking Legal Advice:

- **Consult with a Legal Professional:** If you have doubts or questions about an NDA, it's wise to seek advice from a legal expert. They can help clarify terms and advise on potential risks.
- **Before Disclosing Information:** If you're considering sharing information that might be covered under an NDA, consult a lawyer first. They can guide you on the legality of such disclosure and potential risks.

By understanding the severe implications of breaking an NDA, artists can navigate their professional relationships with greater awareness and caution. This knowledge helps them make informed decisions, respect confidentiality agreements, and maintain professional integrity in the art world.

End-of-Chapter Summary:

Understanding and respecting NDAs is crucial in the professional art world. This chapter, enhanced with insights into the legal repercussions of breaking an NDA, underscores their importance and the need for careful consideration before entering these agreements. As an artist, being informed about the implications of these legal documents ensures you protect not only confidential information but also your professional integrity and legal standing.

NDA
DO'S & DONT'S

DO'S

1 Read and Understand the NDA
Ensure you fully understand the terms before signing. If needed, seek legal advice.

2 Keep Information Confidential
Protect any confidential information shared under the NDA as if it were your own.

3 Follow Duration Terms
Adhere to the time frame specified in the NDA. Confidentiality doesn't end when the project does.

4 Use Information Appropriately
Only use the confidential information for the purpose it was disclosed to you.

5 Report Breaches Immediately
If you suspect a breach of the NDA, report it to the necessary parties as soon as possible.

DON'TS

1 Don't Share Information Indiscriminately
Avoid discussing confidential details with anyone not covered by the NDA.

2 Don't Ignore the Scope
Don't use the confidential information for any purpose other than what's clearly specified in the NDA.

3 Don't Keep Doubts to Yourself
If unsure about the confidentiality of certain information, ask before disclosing it.

4 Don't Forget to Secure Data
Implement proper security measures to protect any confidential information in your possession.

5 Don't Overlook the Consequences
Be aware of the legal and professional consequences of violating the NDA.

~

Interactive Scenario:

Navigating NDA Challenges

- **Scenario Title:** The Tempting Offer
- **Background:** You, an emerging visual artist, have recently signed an NDA with a well-known art gallery, "Modern Visions." The gallery has commissioned you to create a unique installation piece for an upcoming and highly secretive exhibition. The details of this exhibition, including your involvement and the themes, are strictly confidential as per the NDA.
- **Situation:** A few weeks into the project, you attend a local art networking event. There, you meet Alex, a journalist who specializes in covering the contemporary art scene. Alex has heard rumors about Modern Visions' upcoming exhibition and is eager to get an insider's perspective for an exclusive story. They offer you significant publicity in a renowned art magazine in exchange for some details about the exhibition.

Decision Points:

1. **Share Limited Information:** You consider sharing just enough information to pique interest without revealing critical details of the exhibition.
2. **Decline Politely:** You politely decline to share information, citing a confidentiality agreement.

3. **Offer Alternative Information:** Instead of discussing the exhibition, you offer to share about your general artistic process or past projects that are already public.

Questions for Consideration:

- What are the potential consequences of each decision on your relationship with Modern Visions and your future career opportunities?
- How might each choice align with or violate the terms of your NDA?
- **Task:** Decide how you would handle this situation and discuss the reasoning behind your choice. Consider the implications of breaking the NDA against the potential benefits of Alex's publicity.

Chapter 3 Quiz: Understanding NDA Repercussions

1. What can be a potential consequence of breaching an NDA?

A) Loss of reputation

B) Legal action and financial damages

C) Increased publicity

D) All of the above

2. What should you do first if you unintentionally disclose information covered under an NDA?

A) Ignore it and hope no one notices

B) Inform the party who issued the NDA

C) Publicly apologize

D) Delete all evidence of the disclosure

3. Can discussing confidential information with family or friends violate an NDA?

A) Yes, always

B) No, never

C) Only if they tell others

D) Only if they are in the same industry

4. What is NOT usually covered by an NDA?

A) Publicly available information

B) Trade secrets

C) Unreleased product designs

D) Financial information

5. What's the best practice before signing an NDA?

A) Sign it immediately to show trust

B) Have it reviewed by a legal professional

C) Ask for opinions on social media

D) Copy the terms for your use

Answer Key:

1. B) Legal action and financial damages

2. B) Inform the party who issued the NDA

3. A) Yes, always

4. A) Publicly available information

5. B) Have it reviewed by a legal professional

4

NEGOTIATING CONTRACTS
AND NDAS

Mastering the Art of Legal Negotiation

N egotiation is an art in itself, requiring as much finesse and skill as creating your artwork. In "Mastering the Art of Legal Negotiation," we will explore how you, as an artist, can navigate through negotiations of contracts and NDAs, ensuring that your rights are protected and your artistic vision is respected.

1. Preparing for Negotiation

- Explanation: The importance of preparation before entering any negotiation.
- In Practice: Research the party you're negotiating with, understand the value of your work, and know your non-negotiable terms.
- Key Considerations: Setting clear goals and understanding your leverage.

2. Negotiation Tactics and Strategies

- <u>Explanation</u>: Different strategies to employ during negotiations, tailored to various scenarios in the art world.
- <u>In Practice</u>: Tactics for negotiating payment terms, intellectual property rights, and creative control.
- <u>Key Considerations</u>: Understanding when to compromise and when to stand firm.

Cultural Considerations in Negotiations: As the art world is increasingly global, understanding cultural differences in negotiation styles is crucial. Different cultures may have varying approaches to communication, decision-making, and agreement terms. For instance, some cultures might value directness and speed, while others prefer a more relationship-focused and gradual negotiation process. Being sensitive to these differences and adapting your approach can significantly enhance your negotiation success in an international context.

3. Communicating Effectively

- <u>Explanation</u>: How clear communication can make or break a negotiation.
- <u>In Practice</u>: Articulate your points clearly, listen actively, and navigate difficult conversations.
- <u>Key Considerations</u>: Avoiding misunderstandings and building a foundation for long-term professional relationships.

4. Closing the Deal

- <u>Explanation</u>: Finalize a negotiation and ensure that the agreement reflects the mutually agreed terms.

- In Practice: Reviewing the contract post-negotiation, ensuring all negotiated terms are accurately documented. If it's not written in the contract, it was never agreed to.
- Key Considerations: When and how to walk away if the terms are unfavorable.

Case Examples of Successful Art Negotiations:

To illustrate the application of these strategies in real-life scenarios, consider the following cases:

- **Case 1: Gallery Representation:** An emerging artist successfully negotiated a higher commission percentage with a gallery by highlighting their growing popularity and recent successful shows.

- **Case 2: Public Art Commission:** A street artist negotiated a higher budget for a mural project by demonstrating the additional community engagement and publicity value their work would bring.

- **Case 3: Collaboration Contract:** Two artists working on a collaborative installation used a cooperative negotiation approach to ensure both had equal creative input and fair profit sharing.

End-of-Chapter Summary:

Negotiating contracts and NDAs can be challenging, but with the proper preparation and skills, it can also be incredibly empowering. This chapter will equip you with the tools and confidence to navigate these discussions, ensuring your artistic and professional interests are well-represented and protected.

~

Role-Playing Exercise - Mock Negotiation Scenario

Scenario Title: Negotiating an Art Commission Agreement

- **Background:** You have been approached by a local business, "Cafe Artisto," to create a large mural on their main wall. They have a vision for the mural but are open to your artistic interpretation. They have proposed a budget that you feel undervalues your work and effort.

Roles:

- **Artist:** You will play yourself, the artist being commissioned.
- **Cafe Owner:** A friend or colleague can play the role of the cafe owner who wants to commission the mural.

Objective:

- Negotiate a fair price for the mural that reflects the value of your work.
- Discuss and agree upon the artistic direction, timeline, and any additional terms (e.g., maintenance, ownership rights).

Preparation:

- Review the initial proposal from Cafe Artisto.
- Prepare your counteroffer, including your desired fee and any other terms you wish to negotiate.
- Plan your negotiation strategy, considering the skills and tactics discussed in the chapter.

Mock Negotiation Flow:

1. **Initial Meeting:** Begin negotiating with the cafe owner, discussing the project details and their initial offer.
2. **Presenting Your Counteroffer:** Introduce your counteroffer, highlighting your rationale for the desired fee and terms.
3. **Handling Objections:** Respond to any objections or concerns the cafe owner raises, aiming for a mutually beneficial solution.
4. **Reaching Agreement:** Work towards an agreement that satisfies both parties, focusing on collaborative problem-solving.
5. **Finalizing Terms:** Conclude the negotiation by summarizing the agreed-upon terms and discussing the next steps.

Debrief:

- After the role-play, reflect on the negotiation process.
- Discuss what strategies worked well and what could be improved.
- Consider how the skills practiced in this exercise can be applied in actual negotiations.

~

Negotiation Checklist

Before Entering Any Negotiation, Consider the Following:

1. Understand Your Objectives:

- Identify your primary goals for the negotiation.
- Determine your non-negotiables and what aspects you are willing to compromise on.

2. Research the Other Party:

- Learn about the party you will negotiate with (their interests, previous deals, reputation).
- Understand their potential needs and goals in the negotiation.
- Consider independently researching or asking the client for references from previous artistic collaborations, enabling you to gain firsthand insights about their reliability and professionalism.

3. Know Your Worth:

- Assess the value of your work or contribution.
- Be ready to articulate this value convincingly.

4. Prepare Your Proposal:

- Develop a clear proposal or counterproposal that outlines your terms.
- Ensure it aligns with your objectives and values.

5. Understand the Legal Implications:

- Be aware of the legal aspects of what you negotiate (contracts, rights, royalties).
- If necessary, consult with a legal professional beforehand.

6. Plan for Different Scenarios:

- Consider different outcomes and how you would respond to them.
- Prepare for possible objections or counteroffers.

7. Develop Key Talking Points:

- Outline the main points you want to discuss or negotiate.
- Practice articulating these points clearly and confidently.

8. Set the Right Tone:

- Decide on the tone and approach for the negotiation (collaborative, assertive, etc.).
- Plan how to build rapport and establish a positive negotiation environment.

9. Plan Your Strategy:

- Determine your negotiation strategy and tactics.
- Decide when to present certain information or arguments.

10. Prepare for Compromise:

- Identify areas where you are willing to be flexible.
- Consider what concessions you can offer to reach a mutually beneficial agreement.

11. Know Your Exit Strategy:

- Decide in advance under what conditions you would walk away from the negotiation.
- Have a clear plan for ending the negotiation if it does not meet your minimum requirements.

12. Arrange Logistics:

- Ensure you have a comfortable and suitable location for the negotiation.
- Plan for sufficient time to discuss all necessary points without rushing.

5

COMMON PITFALLS AND HOW TO
AVOID THEM

Navigating Legal Pitfalls in the Art World

The path of an artist is often strewn with legal complexities that can be as intricate as the art itself. In this chapter, "Navigating Legal Pitfalls in the Art World," we aim to illuminate these common legal challenges and provide you with the knowledge and tools to avoid them, safeguarding your art and career.

1. Understanding Contractual Obligations

- Explanation: The importance of fully understanding all contractual obligations before signing.
- In Practice: Case studies highlighting artists who faced difficulties due to overlooked contract clauses.
- Key Considerations: Always read and understand every part of a contract, and don't hesitate to seek clarification or legal advice.

2. Protecting Intellectual Property

- <u>Explanation</u>: Common mistakes artists make that can jeopardize their intellectual property rights.
- <u>In Practice</u>: Examples of intellectual property disputes and how they could have been avoided.
- <u>Key Considerations</u>: Be proactive in protecting your work and understand the scope of your intellectual property rights.

Global Legal Variances in Art Law: The legal landscape for artists varies significantly across countries. Depending on the jurisdiction, intellectual property laws, contract enforcement, and digital rights can have different interpretations and legal consequences. It's essential for artists engaging in international projects or selling their art globally to be aware of these variances. In such cases, consulting with legal professionals with expertise in international art law is advisable to ensure compliance with local laws and effectively navigate any cross-border legal challenges.

3. Managing Client Expectations

- <u>Explanation</u>: The risks of miscommunication or misunderstanding with clients.
- <u>In Practice</u>: Scenarios where unclear communication led to legal disputes and how to prevent such situations.
- <u>Key Considerations</u>: Clear and consistent communication is critical; document all agreements and discussions.

4. Avoiding Infringement

- <u>Explanation</u>: The danger of inadvertently infringing on someone else's intellectual property.

- <u>In Practice</u>: How to ensure your work is original and not infringing on existing artworks or copyrights.
- <u>Key Considerations</u>: Conduct thorough research and, if in doubt, seek legal counsel.

Case Studies of Artists Navigating Legal Pitfalls:

- **Case Study 1: Overcoming Copyright Disputes:** A digital artist created a series of works that gained popularity online. Another artist copied these works, claiming they were inspired by them. The original artist successfully challenged this through legal action, setting a precedent for copyright protection in digital art.
- **Case Study 2: Successful Contract Negotiation:** An artist was offered an exhibition contract with a clause that excessively restricted the future display of their works. The artist secured more favorable terms by negotiating this clause, ensuring their artistic freedom and future exhibition opportunities.

These cases illustrate the importance of being vigilant and proactive in legal matters. They show how understanding your rights and seeking appropriate legal counsel can help navigate and resolve potential legal issues in an artist's career.

Emerging Challenges in the Digital Art Space

Navigating the World of NFTs

1. Digital Copyright and NFTs:

- **Understanding the Intersection:** Learn how copyright law applies to NFTs and digital artworks. Recognize the legal implications of creating, buying, and selling NFTs.
- **Action Steps for Artists:**
- Research and understand the fundamentals of NFTs and how they are used in the digital art market.

- Consult with legal experts to understand the copyright aspects of NFTs before creating or selling them.
- Ensure clarity in smart contracts associated with NFTs to define precisely what rights are being sold or retained.

2. Case Studies: Legal Disputes in Digital Art and NFTs:

- **Learning from Real Cases:** Analyze real-world legal disputes involving NFTs to understand common pitfalls and how to avoid them.
- **Practical Application for Artists:**
- Review and learn from these case studies to recognize potential legal challenges you might face with NFTs.
- Apply these learnings to your practices, particularly in protecting your rights when engaging with NFTs.

Case Study: New Media Arts – Digital Art and NFTs

- **Background:** A digital artist created a series of artworks and sold them as NFTs. However, buyers were unclear about what they were purchasing – the digital image or the NFT.
- **Legal Focus:** Understanding the legalities and rights transferred in NFT transactions.
- **Outcome:** The artist had to clarify the terms, emphasizing the distinction between owning the NFT and the copyright of the digital art itself.

3. Understanding the Digital Landscape:

- **Keeping Up with Digital Advancements:** Stay informed about the rapidly evolving world of digital art and NFTs.
- **Steps for Artists:**
- Regularly follow industry news and updates on digital art and NFTs.

- Participate in forums, workshops, or webinars to stay updated on legal developments in the NFT space.
- Network with other artists and legal experts to share experiences and strategies for navigating the NFT market.

4. Seeking Expert Advice:

- **Consulting with Specialists:** Engage with legal professionals specializing in digital art and NFTs for personalized advice.
- **How Artists Benefit:**
- Gain tailored advice on your specific NFT projects or plans.
- Understand the nuances of NFT contracts and transactions to make informed decisions.

Deep Dive into Digital Art

- **Understanding the Medium:** Digital art varies in form and function. Familiarize yourself with software and hardware tools that enhance your artistic capabilities.
- **Rights and Reproductions:** The ease of duplication in digital art requires stringent rights management. Be clear about the terms when selling or licensing your digital artwork.
- **Engaging Audiences:** Digital art often reaches a broader audience faster. Utilize social media and digital galleries to showcase your work.

Best Practices for Digital Artists

- **Protecting Your Work:** Implement strategies to protect your digital artwork, such as watermarking and using secure platforms to showcase it.
- **Marketing Your Digital Art:** Develop an online presence tailored to your digital art. Engage with digital art communities, participate in online exhibitions, and leverage social media.
- **Staying Informed:** The digital art landscape is evolving rapidly. Stay updated on the latest trends, tools, and legal developments.

Case Studies on Digital Art and NFTs

Digital Artist's Journey with NFTs: A digital artist creates a unique animated piece and decides to sell it as an NFT. They navigate through minting, pricing, and selling the NFT, learning about the importance of community engagement in the NFT space and the nuances of digital ownership.

End-of-Chapter Summary:

As we navigate the evolving landscape of the art world, marked by rapid digital innovation and the rise of new mediums like NFTs, we encounter a spectrum of challenges and opportunities. This chapter, focusing on emerging issues in digital copyrights and NFTs, has provided you with the essential knowledge to confidently maneuver through the digital art space, fully aware of its legal implications.

THE INSIGHTS SHARED HERE UNDERSCORE the importance of understanding copyright in the context of NFTs, learning from real-world legal disputes, and staying abreast of digital advancements. This understanding is crucial for safeguarding your artistic creations and rights in the digital era and exploring new opportunities with an explicit and informed perspective.

SIMULTANEOUSLY, this chapter has highlighted the significance of recognizing and avoiding common legal pitfalls. By being proactive and well-informed, you can steer your artistic career towards greater confidence and security. Prevention in legal matters is always more advantageous than seeking remedies after issues arise. Equipped with the tools and insights provided in this chapter, you can protect your art, uphold your reputation, and maintain peace of mind.

WHETHER DEALING with traditional art mediums or venturing into the frontiers of digital art and NFTs, staying informed, vigilant, and adaptive is essential. The art world is dynamic, so should your approach to navigating its legal aspects. By embracing these principles, you are well-prepared to navigate your artistic journey in the art world with assurance, clarity, and a sense of empowerment.

~

Digital Art Legal Scenarios

Scenario 1: The Digital Artwork Reproduction

Background: You discover that your digital artwork, which you sold as a limited edition, is being reproduced and sold by an unauthorized online retailer. The retailer argues that digital works are not subject to traditional copyright laws.

- **Task:**
- Decide how to address the unauthorized reproduction.
- Consider contacting the retailer, issuing a cease-and-desist, or seeking legal action.
- Reflect on how copyright law applies to digital artwork and the importance of DRM (Digital Rights Management).

Scenario 2: The NFT Royalty Dispute

Background: You sold an artwork as an NFT, with a contract stating that you would receive a percentage of sales each time the NFT is resold. However, the current holder of the NFT sold it privately, bypassing the platform that enforces the royalty agreement.

- **Task:**
- Evaluate your options for enforcing the royalty agreement.
- Explore legal and practical steps to claim your royalties.
- Discuss the challenges in enforcing contracts within the NFT marketplace.

Scenario 3: The Collaborative Digital Project

Background: You are part of a collaborative digital art project. A dispute arose over the ownership and distribution rights of the final digital work, as there was no formal agreement outlining each contributor's rights.

- **Task:**
- Propose a resolution that respects the rights of all collaborators.
- Consider creating a retrospective agreement to clarify rights and distribution.
- Emphasize the importance of clear agreements in collaborative digital projects.

Scenario 4: The Viral Artwork Misuse

Background: One of your digital artworks goes viral on social media. You find that various businesses are using it for promotional purposes without your permission or credit.

- **Task:**
- Decide how to respond to the unauthorized commercial use of your artwork.
- Assess the steps to protect your work and claim compensation or credit.
- Reflect on strategies to monitor and control the use of your digital art online.

~

Discussion Points on the Future of Digital Art

Objective: Encourage artists to critically explore the evolving landscape of digital art, including legal aspects and potential opportunities.

Discussion Points:

1. Impact of Digital Technologies:

- How are emerging digital technologies like VR, AR, and AI reshaping the creation and consumption of art?
- How do these technologies challenge traditional notions of art ownership and copyright?

2. Legal Challenges in the Digital Realm:

- What unique legal challenges might artists face when creating and selling digital art?
- How does the law need to adapt to address issues specific to digital art, such as replication and distribution?

3. The Rise of NFTs:

- How do Non-Fungible Tokens (NFTs) alter the landscape for digital artists?
- What legal considerations should artists be aware of when creating or investing in NFTs?

4. Online Art Platforms and Marketplaces:

- How do online platforms and marketplaces impact artists' ability to reach audiences and monetize their work?
- What legal precautions should artists take when engaging with these platforms?

5. Digital Art and Intellectual Property:

- How does the digital format affect artists' ability to protect their intellectual property?
- Discuss the balance between sharing art online for exposure and protecting it from unauthorized use or reproduction.

6. Ethical Considerations in Digital Art:

- What ethical questions arise with using AI and other technologies in art creation?
- How can artists navigate these ethical considerations while embracing digital innovation?

7. Future of Digital Art:

- What do you envision for the future of digital art in terms of creative possibilities and legal frameworks?
- How can artists prepare themselves for the legal realities of an increasingly digital art world?

~

Pitfall Prevention Plan

Objective: To assist artists in proactively identifying and mitigating potential legal risks in their art projects, both traditional and digital.

Pitfall Prevention Plan Template:

1. Project Description:

- Briefly describe your art project, including the medium, scope, and intended platform or venue for display/sale.

2. Identify Potential Legal Risks:

- List any legal concerns that might be relevant to your project (copyright infringement, contract disputes, NFT legality, etc.).

3. Risk Assessment:

- For each identified risk, assess its likelihood and potential impact on your project.

4. Legal Compliance:

- Review relevant laws and regulations that apply to your project.
- Check for specific legal requirements for your art medium or the platform you intend to use.

5. Contractual Agreements:

- Outline the vital contractual agreements required if working with galleries, collaborators, or clients.
- Highlight any clauses that need careful attention (e.g., intellectual property rights, payment terms).

6. Intellectual Property Strategy:

- Plan how to protect your intellectual property (copyright registration, watermarking digital work, etc.).
- Consider any permissions or licenses needed if incorporating others' work.

7. Digital Art Specifics:

- If applicable, address specific risks associated with digital art (file security, replication, blockchain verification for NFTs).

8. Mitigation Strategies:

- For each identified risk, develop strategies to mitigate or manage it.
- Include contingency plans for unforeseen legal issues.

9. Professional Consultation:

- List any aspects where professional legal advice might be required.
- Schedule consultations with legal experts, especially for complex or high-stakes projects.

10. Documentation and Record-Keeping:

- Plan for a thorough documentation of your creative process, contracts, and any legal steps taken.
- Keep records organized for easy access in case of legal disputes.

11. Review and Update:

- Regularly review and update your prevention plan, especially as your project evolves or new legal developments arise.

Chapter 5 Quiz: Legal Pitfalls in Digital and Traditional Art

1. Which of the following is a common legal pitfall in digital art sales?

A) Incorrect framing of artwork

B) Failure to verify the authenticity of a digital certificate

C) Inadequate lighting in a gallery

D) Overpricing artwork

2. What is a critical legal consideration when creating NFTs?

A) Ensuring physical delivery of the artwork

B) Verifying blockchain authenticity

C) Obtaining performance rights

D) Using eco-friendly materials

3. In traditional art contracts, what can be a significant pitfall?

A) Not defining the digital resolution

B) Ignoring the scope of work clause

C) Failing to consider online platforms

D) Neglecting the color palette used

4. What should artists be cautious of in online art marketplaces?

A) Personal taste of the audience

B) Color calibration of monitors

C) Copyright infringement risks

D) Choosing the right frame

5. How can artists protect themselves from unauthorized reproduction of their digital artwork?

A) Regularly changing their artistic style

B) Using watermarks and digital rights management (DRM)

C) Only displaying art in physical galleries

D) Avoiding the use of popular themes

Answer Key:

1. B) Failure to verify the authenticity of a digital certificate

2. B) Verifying blockchain authenticity

3. B) Ignoring the scope of work clause

4. C) Copyright infringement risks

5. B) Using watermarks and digital rights management

6

PROTECTING YOUR RIGHTS AS AN ARTIST

Safeguarding Your Creative Legacy

Y our art is not just a product of your creativity; it's a legacy that carries your unique signature. In "Safeguarding Your Creative Legacy," this chapter is devoted to helping you understand and protect the rights that preserve the integrity and value of your work. It's about turning your artistic expression into a lasting legacy.

1. Understanding Copyrights in Depth

- Explanation: A deep dive into copyright laws and how they apply specifically to your artwork.
- In Practice: Real-life examples of artists who successfully defended their copyrights or, conversely, cases where they were infringed upon.
- Key Considerations: How to register your work and what to do in case of infringement.

Case Study: Performing Arts – Copyright and Choreography

- **Background:** A renowned choreographer created a unique dance sequence for a theater production. A video of the performance was uploaded online and went viral. Another theater company then replicated the choreography in their show without permission.
- **Legal Focus:** Copyright infringement in choreography.
- **Outcome:** The original choreographer filed a lawsuit for copyright infringement and won. The case highlighted the importance of copyright protection for choreographic works.

Global Perspective on Copyright Laws:

Artists must recognize that copyright laws vary significantly around the world. While the principles might be similar, the specifics can differ in duration, scope, and enforcement. For instance, some countries offer more robust protections for moral rights than others. Understanding these differences is vital when engaging in international projects or distributing your work globally. Consider consulting with legal experts knowledgeable in international copyright law to ensure your work is protected no matter where it reaches.

2. Moral Rights and Their Importance

- Explanation: What are moral rights, and why are they crucial for artists?
- In Practice: Scenarios where moral rights have played a key role in protecting an artist's reputation and work.
- Key Considerations: Understanding your rights to attribution and integrity of your work.

Case Study: Sculpture – Public Display and Moral Rights

- **Background:** A sculptor sold a prominent outdoor sculpture to a city. Years later, the city decided to paint the sculpture in a public beautification initiative, altering its original look.
- **Legal Focus:** Moral rights of the artist, specifically the right to integrity of the work.
- **Outcome:** The artist successfully argued that their moral rights were infringed, leading to the restoration of the sculpture to its original state.

Case Studies of Artists Asserting Their Rights:

- **Traditional Medium Case Study:** A major fashion brand reproduced An artist's painting without their consent. The artist successfully sued for copyright infringement, highlighting the importance of vigilance and legal action in protecting one's work.
- **Digital Art Case Study:** A digital artist found their work being used in an online advertising campaign. They negotiated a licensing deal that compensated them fairly and led to further collaborations, demonstrating the potential for constructive resolution in copyright disputes.

These cases illustrate the effectiveness of understanding and actively managing your legal rights as an artist, whether working with traditional media or navigating the digital art world.

3. Licensing Agreements: Sharing Your Work Wisely

- Explanation: How to structure licensing agreements that respect your rights and intentions.
- In Practice: Case studies on effective licensing strategies and common pitfalls to avoid.
- Key Considerations: Negotiating terms that align with your creative and financial goals.

4. Dealing with Infringements and Disputes

- Explanation: Steps to take when your rights are
  challenged or infringed upon.
- In Practice: Guidance on resolving disputes, whether
  through negotiation, mediation, or legal action.
- Key Considerations: The importance of documentation
  and seeking professional advice.

Copyright Registration and Its Importance

The Rule of Thumb: Register Everything

While it's true that your artwork is automatically protected by copyright upon creation, registering your work with the U.S. Copyright
Office significantly bolsters your legal protections. Here's why and
when you should consider registering:

Why Register Your Copyright:

- **Stronger Legal Standing:** Registered works offer a higher
  level of protection, especially in infringement disputes. If
  your work is registered, you are eligible for statutory
  damages and attorney's fees in court, which is not the case
  with unregistered works.
- **Public Record:** Registration creates a public record of
  your copyright, which can be beneficial in proving
  ownership.
- **Deterrence of Infringement:** The fact that a work is
  registered can deter potential infringers.

When to Register:

- **As Soon as Possible:** Ideally, register your artwork as soon as it's completed and before it is published or distributed.
- **Before Public Exposure:** If you plan to showcase your work publicly, ensure it is registered beforehand. This is crucial for works that might appear in places where they could be easily copied or used without permission, such as online platforms, galleries, or public installations.
- **Continuous Process:** Register new works regularly, mainly if you produce a significant volume of art.

Dealing with Infringement:

- If you discover your work being used without permission, such as in advertisements or TV shows, having a registered copyright simplifies the process of taking legal action.
- While there are exceptions like "de minimis" use, these can be complex and fact-specific. Registered works generally afford you a stronger position in any legal dispute.

How to Register:

- Visit the U.S. Copyright Office website for the registration process, which can be completed online.
- There is a registration fee, but it's a worthwhile investment for the legal protection it offers.

Remember: Though there is an inherent copyright in each piece of work you create, having formal registration provides tangible proof of ownership and a more robust legal basis for protecting your rights. In the complex world of art and copyright, being proactive about registration is a wise and beneficial strategy.

Copyright and Photography of Artwork

Understanding the Implications of Photographing Artwork

A common legal misunderstanding in the art world involves the rights associated with photographs of artwork. While the photographer holds the copyright to their photo, this does not automatically grant them unrestricted rights to use or sell the photograph if it prominently features another artist's work. Here's what you need to know:

1. Artwork as the Main Subject:

- If your artwork is the primary subject of a photograph, the selling or commercial use can infringe upon your copyright.
- Your rights limit the photographer's rights to use the image commercially as the original artist.

2. Photography for Commercial Use:

- For a photograph of your artwork to be used commercially (such as in advertisements or merchandise), the photographer must obtain your permission or license.
- This applies even if the photograph itself is an original creation of the photographer.

3. Fair Use and Exceptions:

- There are certain exceptions under the fair use doctrine, such as for educational purposes, criticism, news reporting, or scholarly research, where the photograph might be used without the artist's permission.
- However, these exceptions are specific and must meet certain legal criteria.

4. Protecting Your Rights:

- Be proactive in addressing issues where your artwork is photographed and used without your consent.
- Consider including clauses in your contracts or agreements regarding the photography and use of your work.

5. Seeking Legal Advice:

- If you are still determining the rights and permissions associated with photographs of your artwork, particularly for commercial purposes, it is advisable to seek legal counsel.

Selling Your Copyright

The Implications of Signing Away Copyright

Understanding Copyright: Copyright is a legal right that grants the creator of original work exclusive rights to its use and distribution, typically for the creator's lifetime plus a number of years (varying by jurisdiction). This includes the right to reproduce, distribute, display, perform, and create derivative works from the original artwork.

. . .

WHAT IT MEANS **to Sign Away Copyright:** When artists sign away their copyright, they transfer these exclusive rights to another individual or entity. This means:

1. **Loss of Control:** The artist no longer controls how the artwork is used, reproduced, or displayed. The new copyright owner can modify, sell, or destroy the work without the original artist's consent.
2. **Financial Implications:** The artist may lose out on potential future earnings from the artwork. Once the copyright is transferred, the artist has no claim to royalties or profits from the work's use.
3. **Duration:** The transfer is often in perpetuity, meaning it lasts for the work's copyright term, which can be the artist's lifetime plus several decades.

Pros of Signing Away Copyright:

- **Immediate Financial Benefit:** Artists may receive a substantial upfront payment for their copyright.
- **Exposure:** If the buyer has significant distribution channels or influence, it can lead to greater exposure to the artist's work.
- **Simplicity:** It eliminates the need to manage or enforce the copyright, benefiting artists who prefer to focus solely on the creative process.

Cons of Signing Away Copyright:

- **Loss of Future Revenue:** Potential future profits from the artwork, such as licensing fees or royalties, are relinquished.
- **Loss of Creative Control:** The buyer can alter, license, or otherwise use the artwork without the artist's input or approval.
- **Impact on Artist's Portfolio:** Without permission, the artist may be unable to use the work in personal portfolios or future exhibitions.

Important Considerations:

- **Understand the Terms:** Fully understand any contract's terms involving transferring copyright. Seek legal advice if needed.
- **Negotiate Terms:** Consider negotiating more favorable terms, such as limiting the duration of the transfer or retaining certain rights.
- **Alternatives to Full Transfer:** Explore alternatives like licensing, which allows others to use the artwork while the artist retains copyright.

Pricing Considerations When Selling Copyright:

When considering selling your copyright, pricing it appropriately is crucial. This decision should reflect not only the current value of the artwork but also its potential future value. Here's a framework to help determine a fair price:

1. Evaluate Long-Term Value:

- Assess the potential long-term popularity and demand for your work.
- Consider possible future artwork uses, such as reproductions, merchandise, or digital formats.

2. Estimate Future Earnings:

- Calculate potential future earnings if you were to retain the copyright. This includes royalties, licensing fees, and sales of reproductions.
- Consider the duration of copyright (your lifetime plus several years) for these calculations.

3. Substantial Pricing Increase:

- Given the loss of future earnings and control, price the copyright substantially higher than the current artwork value.
- A common approach is to start with a multiple of the artwork's current selling price (e.g., 3x to 5x), adjusting based on the artwork's uniqueness, your reputation, and potential future value.

4. Market Comparison:

- Research prices for similar copyright transactions in your art genre.
- Understand the standard rates in your industry to ensure competitive pricing.

5. Negotiation Strategy:

- Be prepared to negotiate. Have a clear minimum price in mind, but be open to discussions.
- Consider non-monetary benefits, such as exposure or future collaboration opportunities, as part of the negotiation.

6. Legal Consultation:

- Consult with a legal professional to understand the full implications of the transfer.
- Ensure the contract terms clearly outline the scope and terms of the copyright transfer.

Remember: Selling your copyright is a significant decision that can have long-term implications for your career. It's essential to approach this decision with a thorough understanding of your work's potential and a strategy to ensure you are fairly compensated for both your current artistic contributions and future potential.

Navigating VARA Rights

Understanding VARA:

The Visual Artists Rights Act (VARA) of 1990 is a significant piece of legislation in United States copyright law that grants artists certain rights over their visual artworks, even after these works have been sold. VARA focuses explicitly on artists' moral rights, separate from economic rights (like copyright).

Critical Protections Under VARA:

- Right to Attribution: An artist's right to be recognized as the creator of their work.
- Right to Integrity: The right of an artist to prevent any distortion, mutilation, or other modification of their work that would be prejudicial to their honor or reputation.

Applicability:

- VARA applies to works of 'recognized stature,' which generally means fine art such as paintings, murals, sculptures, drawings, and limited-edition prints.
- These rights are applicable even if the artist no longer owns the artwork.

Duration of VARA Rights:

VARA rights are protected for the author's life plus 70 years for works created on or after June 1, 1991.

Waiver of Rights:

While VARA rights are inherent, the artist can waive them. However, the waiver must be explicit and in writing.

How to Navigate VARA:

- Be Aware: Understand how VARA rights apply to your work and the implications for your art.
- Explicit Agreements: If considering a waiver of VARA rights, ensure it is explicit in writing and that you fully understand the consequences.
- Document Your Work: Keep thorough records of your works and their status regarding VARA rights.

Why VARA Matters:

VARA is crucial for artists who want to maintain the integrity of their work and protect their reputations. It empowers artists to have a say in how their work is treated even after it leaves their studio, ensuring their artistic vision is respected.

Navigating International Opportunities

As the art world increasingly becomes a global marketplace, you may find opportunities to exhibit, collaborate, or sell your artwork internationally. While this manual provides a solid foundation for understanding basic legal concepts, it's essential to recognize that the legal landscape can vary significantly from one country to another.

Key Points to Consider:

- **Complex Legal Variabilities:** International art laws and practices can differ significantly regarding copyright duration, moral rights recognition, and enforcement. These variations can profoundly affect how your art is protected and utilized abroad.

- **Seek Specialized Legal Counsel:** Engage with legal professionals specializing in international art law. They can provide tailored advice and guidance relevant to the specific country or region you're dealing with. This step ensures your rights are comprehensively protected under different legal systems.
- **Build a Global Network:** Connect with other artists and join international art organizations. These networks can be invaluable resources, offering insights, experiences, and support for navigating the global art market. They can also provide recommendations for legal experts in various countries.
- **Stay Informed and Adaptive:** Keep yourself informed about international trends and changes in art law. Being adaptable and knowledgeable about global practices will protect your work and open doors to new opportunities and collaborations.

End-of-Chapter Summary:

Understanding and protecting your rights is fundamental to ensuring your art continues to be a source of pride, reputation, and livelihood. This chapter gives you the knowledge to create, protect, control, and benefit from your creations in the long run.

~

Scenario Analysis: Protecting Your Rights

Scenario 1: The Unauthorized Exhibition

- **Background:** You discover a gallery exhibiting one of your artworks without your permission. The gallery claims they obtained it from a third party and were unaware of the need for your consent.

Decision Points:

1. **Contact the Gallery Directly:** Reach out to the gallery to discuss the situation, assert your copyright, and negotiate terms for the exhibition.
2. **Legal Action:** Initiate legal proceedings against the gallery for copyright infringement.
3. **Public Response:** Use social media to publicize the issue and seek public support to pressure the gallery into compliance.

Questions for Consideration:

- What are the potential risks and benefits of each approach?
- How can you ensure your rights are respected while maintaining professional relationships?

Scenario 2: The Altered Mural

- **Background:** A commissioned mural you created for a local business has been significantly altered without your consent, changing the artwork's original intent and style.

Decision Points:

1. **Negotiate with the Business:** Discuss the alterations with the owner and seek a resolution respecting your moral rights.
2. **Demand Restoration:** Insist that the mural be restored to its original state or removed entirely.
3. **Legal Counsel:** Seek advice from a legal professional on how to proceed with enforcing your moral rights.

Questions for Consideration:

- How do the alterations impact your reputation and the integrity of your work?
- What steps can you take to address the situation while upholding your moral rights?

Scenario 3: The Digital Reproduction Dilemma

- **Background:** You find that a digital artwork you created is being reproduced and sold online by an unknown party.

Decision Points:

1. **Issue a Cease-and-Desist:** Send a formal cease-and-desist letter to the infringing party.

2. **Negotiate Licensing Terms:** Contact the party to negotiate a licensing agreement for the artwork's use.
3. **Report to Online Platforms:** Report the unauthorized sales to the content hosting platforms.

Questions for Consideration:

- How can you effectively enforce your copyright in the digital realm?
- What measures can you take to prevent future unauthorized reproductions of your work?

7

PRACTICAL TIPS FOR ARTISTS

While creativity flows spontaneously, managing the legal aspects of your art requires careful planning and strategy. In "Empowering Your Art with Practical Legal Tools," this chapter is designed to equip you with actionable advice, checklists, and resources that simplify the legal side of your artistic practice, freeing you to focus on what you do best – creating.

NOTE: At the end of this manual, you will find a Contract Review Checklist. This comprehensive checklist is designed to assist you in thoroughly reviewing any artistic contracts you may encounter, ensuring that your interests are well-protected.

1. Contract Review Checklist

- Explanation: A step-by-step guide to reviewing contracts, ensuring you cover all essential aspects.
- In Practice: A real-life example of how an artist used the checklist to negotiate a better contract.

- <u>Key Considerations</u>: Critical clauses to watch out for and common mistakes to avoid.

Real-Life Application:

Example: An emerging photographer was offered an opportunity to exhibit at a local gallery. Before signing the contract, she used the Contract Review Checklist to identify a clause that granted the gallery an excessively long exclusivity period. By recognizing this, she was able to negotiate a shorter period, allowing her greater freedom to exhibit elsewhere. This example underscores the importance of thoroughly reviewing and understanding each contract clause, ensuring they align with your career goals and artistic freedom.

2. Negotiating Royalties and Licensing Agreements

- <u>Explanation</u>: Tips for negotiating fair terms that reflect the value of your work.
- <u>In Practice</u>: Case studies demonstrating successful royalty and licensing negotiations.
- <u>Key Considerations</u>: Balancing immediate financial benefits with long-term gains.

Real-Life Application:

Case Study: A digital artist created a series of illustrations that caught the attention of a major publishing house. The house offered a licensing deal for using the illustrations in an upcoming book series. Initially, the offer included a flat fee with no royalties. Using the knowledge from 'Negotiating Royalties and Licensing Agreements,' the artist successfully negotiated a contract that included a 15% royalty on all sales and the initial fee. This negotiation provided immediate financial benefits and ensured ongoing income as the book series gained popularity.

3. Managing Artistic Collaborations

- <u>Explanation</u>: Best practices for legal arrangements in collaborative projects.

- <u>In Practice</u>: Scenarios where clear legal agreements benefited (or could have benefited) collaborative endeavors.
- <u>Key Considerations</u>: Defining roles, responsibilities, and profit-sharing in collaborations.

Case Study: Mixed Media Art – Collaborative Work and Copyright

- **Background:** Two artists, a painter and a digital artist, collaborated on a mixed-media project. Disputes arose later over copyright ownership and revenue sharing from the project's sales.
- **Legal Focus:** Copyright ownership and profit-sharing in collaborative mixed-media projects.
- **Outcome:** The dispute was settled out of court, with both artists agreeing to share copyright and profits. This case underscored the need for clear agreements in collaborative scenarios.

NOTE: To facilitate successful and legally sound collaborations, I've included a sample Collaboration Agreement Template in the Appendices that can be used as a starting point. Tailor it to fit the specifics of your collaborative project and ensure that all parties clearly understand and agree to the terms.

4. Seeking Legal Advice

- <u>Explanation</u>: When and how to seek professional legal advice.
- <u>In Practice</u>: Insights into how legal counsel has helped artists in complex situations.
- <u>Key Considerations</u>: Finding the right legal advisor for your artistic needs.

Negotiating Royalties and Licensing

Standard Industry Rates:

1. Art Licensing for Merchandise:

- Standard royalties for artwork used on merchandise (like apparel, accessories, and home decor) typically range from 5% to 15% of the retail price or 10% to 20% of the wholesale price.
- **Example:** An artist licensing a design for a t-shirt line might negotiate a 12% royalty on the retail price.

2. Print Reproductions and Publishing:

- For print reproductions (like posters, books, and cards), royalties often range from 10% to 15% of the retail price.
- **Example:** A 10% royalty on each copy sold could be negotiated for a book featuring an artist's work.

3. Digital Art and Online Use:

- Royalties for digital use, such as in video games or websites, vary widely. Depending on the usage scope and exposure, a typical range could be 15% to 25%.
- **Example:** An artist licensing artwork for use in a popular video game might negotiate a 20% royalty on sales revenue.

Additionally, discussing and clarifying terms related to royalty accounting is essential. This includes specifying who will maintain sales records, the frequency of royalty payments, and the method of reporting sales figures to the artist. Ensuring these aspects are transparently outlined in the contract helps maintain trust and fairness in the financial arrangement. Such clarity protects both parties' interests and ensures that the artist receives due compensation without ambiguity.

Successful Negotiation Strategies:

1. Research and Benchmarking:

- Before negotiating, research industry standards for similar works and uses. This information can be used as a benchmark in your negotiations.
- **Strategy Example:** An illustrator looked at standard rates for book illustrations before negotiating her contract, ensuring her rates were competitive and fair.

2. Value Proposition:

- Highlight the unique value and appeal of your work. Emphasize aspects like your style's popularity, your following, or any awards you've received.
- **Strategy Example:** A photographer negotiating with a magazine used his recent photography awards as leverage to secure a higher royalty rate.

3. Flexibility and Trade-offs:

- Be flexible and open to trade-offs. For instance, you might accept a lower royalty rate in exchange for a higher upfront payment or more exposure.
- **Strategy Example:** An artist agreed to a lower royalty rate for a large retail chain in exchange for prominent feature

placement and marketing support.

4. Duration and Exclusivity:

- Consider the duration of the licensing agreement and whether it's exclusive. Shorter terms or non-exclusive rights can justify higher royalty rates.
- **Strategy Example:** A graphic designer agreed to a 2-year, non-exclusive licensing agreement with a higher royalty rate, allowing her to license the work elsewhere simultaneously.

5. Escalation Clauses:

- Negotiate escalation clauses where the royalty rate increases after reaching certain sales milestones.
- **Strategy Example:** A musician's licensing deal for a commercial included an escalation clause where the royalty rate increased after the commercial reached 1 million views.

Navigating Online Art Sales and Protecting Digital Rights

With the surge in digital art platforms, artists face unique challenges and opportunities. This section covers key aspects to consider when engaging in online art sales and protecting digital rights.

1. Understanding Online Platforms:

- Familiarize yourself with terms of service and artist agreements on platforms like Etsy, Saatchi Art, or digital art marketplaces.

- Pay close attention to how these platforms handle copyright and licensing of your work.

2. Digital Rights Management:

- Utilize digital rights management tools to protect your artwork from unauthorized reproduction or use.
- Consider watermarking or using low-resolution images for online display.

3. Handling Disputes:

- Learn the process for addressing copyright infringement or misrepresentation on online platforms.
- Know your rights regarding having your work removed or appropriately credited.

4. Maximizing Exposure While Protecting Your Work:

- Balance the need for exposure with the protection of your digital artwork.
- Strategize on how to use online platforms effectively without compromising your rights.

Intellectual Property Monitoring

Strategies for Monitoring Your Intellectual Property Online

In an era where digital art can be easily shared and reproduced, it's crucial to monitor the use of your work online. This section offers strategies and tools to help artists manage their intellectual property.

1. Utilizing Monitoring Tools:

- Explore tools like Google Alerts, TinEye, or Pixsy for monitoring the online use of your artwork.
- These tools can notify you when your work appears on new websites or is used in ways you haven't authorized.

2. Taking Action Against Unauthorized Use:

- Learn the steps to take when you discover unauthorized use of your work, including cease-and-desist letters and DMCA takedown notices.
- Understand when seeking legal action versus negotiating a licensing agreement is appropriate.

3. Maintaining a Digital Portfolio:

- Keep an up-to-date digital portfolio with artwork records, including creation dates and publication history.
- This portfolio can serve as evidence in case of copyright disputes.

End-of-Chapter Summary:

With these practical tools and tips, you're not just an artist but an informed and legally savvy creator. This chapter aims to streamline the legal aspects of your work, helping you make informed decisions that protect your interests and foster your artistic growth.

REMEMBER: A detailed Contract Review Checklist is available at the end of this manual. This tool will guide you through the critical aspects of contract analysis, helping you to approach contract negotiations and reviews with greater confidence and clarity.

~

Interactive Case Studies

Case Study 1: The Online Art Sale Dispute

Background: You sold a digital artwork through an online art platform. The buyer now claims that the artwork they received does not match the description and is demanding a refund, alleging misrepresentation.

Task:

- Analyze the sales agreement and communication records.
- Determine the best course of action: offer a refund, negotiate a resolution, or defend your position.
- Consider what steps could have been taken to prevent this dispute.

Case Study 2: The Collaborative Exhibition Conflict

Background: You entered into a collaborative project with another artist for an exhibition. However, disagreements have arisen over the division of responsibilities and the sharing of profits. There was no formal agreement drawn up before the collaboration.

Task:

- Assess how to navigate this conflict without damaging professional relationships.
- Propose a fair profit-sharing model and division of responsibilities.

- Reflect on the importance of having a formal collaboration agreement and how it could have mitigated these issues. **Always, always, always put EVERYTHING in writing.**

Case Study 3: Copyright Infringement on Social Media

Background: You discover that one of your paintings has been reproduced and is being used as a promotional image on a company's social media page without your permission.

Task:

- Decide on an initial response: contacting the company directly, issuing a cease-and-desist letter, or seeking legal advice.
- Consider the potential impacts of each action on your reputation and future business opportunities.
- Discuss how copyright registration and monitoring of your work's use could be beneficial.

Case Study 4: Gallery Representation Agreement Review

Background: A well-known art gallery has offered to represent you. They have provided a representation agreement that includes clauses on exclusivity, commission rates, and the promotion of your work.

Task:

- Review the agreement and identify any clauses that may need negotiation or clarification.
- Discuss the implications of the exclusivity clause on your ability to exhibit and sell your work elsewhere.

- Outline a plan for negotiating more favorable terms or addressing any concerns.

CONCLUSION
EMPOWERING YOUR ARTISTIC JOURNEY

Embracing Legal Mastery in Art

As we conclude this exploration of art and law, remember that the insights you've garnered are not mere words; they are the keys to unlocking your full potential as an artist in the legal realm. "Empowering Artistry: Navigating the Legal Landscape" was meticulously crafted to equip and inspire you.

Reflecting on the Journey:

Legal Empowerment: The tools and understanding you now possess are pivotal for safeguarding your work and asserting your rights.

Community and Advocacy: As a member of the vibrant artistic community, share this enlightenment, bolster fellow artists, and champion equitable practices in the art world.

Evolving with the Art World: The art domain is in perpetual motion, and legalities are evolving alongside it. Nurture your curiosity, stay informed, and embrace growth in your artistic and legal acumen.

Looking Forward:

Your art mirrors your unique essence and message. Continue crafting and sharing your art, fortified with legal savvy and protection. Let the wisdom from this manual underpin a flourishing and resilient artistic career.

Adapting to Future Trends:

The legal contours of the art world are ever-changing, especially with the digital revolution and new art mediums. Embrace adaptability and a commitment to lifelong learning. Engage with evolving technologies, delve into emerging art forms, and proactively understand their legal frameworks.

Stay connected with the latest art law through workshops, artist networks, and consultations with legal professionals. Your art is an invaluable cultural and societal asset deserving robust protection and advocacy.

Remember, your art transcends being just a legacy; it's a vital thread in the fabric of human expression. Armed with knowledge, confidence, and adaptability, your impact on the art world is boundless today and into the future.

Final Encouragement:

Step into your artistic endeavors with renewed confidence and clarity. Let your creativity soar, secure in knowing your rights are safeguarded. Here's to a future where your art is not only seen and celebrated but also legally protected and revered.

Mastering Contract Negotiations:

In concluding our legal odyssey, remember a crucial tenet: all elements within a contract are open to negotiation. This guide has empowered you to approach contract discussions with assertiveness and insight. Always ensure the final agreement reflects all negotiated terms, as only these will have legal standing if disputes arise. Your artistic journey combines creativity and professional insight, calling for informed legal engagement and proactive action.

ABOUT THE AUTHOR

About Kesía Ramos

Kesía Ramos is a multifaceted professional with diverse expertise in the arts and business. As the Managing Director and Project Manager at Don Rimx Inc., she has been pivotal in managing the artistic endeavors of renowned artist Don Rimx. Her responsibilities encompass client negotiations and logistical planning for complex art projects. Her collaboration with prominent corporations, including Electronic Arts and Burger King, is a testament to her adaptability and skill.

In 2023, Kesía founded Workflow Guru LLC, offering high-level administrative support to small companies, further showcasing her entrepreneurial spirit and business acumen. Previously, she ventured into vegan beauty with The More Better Brand, demonstrating her ability to identify and pursue emerging market trends. Although this venture has since been dissolved, it speaks volumes about her willingness to take risks and her capacity for innovation.

Kesía's academic journey began with a cum laude degree in Advertising and Marketing Communications from the Fashion Institute of Technology in New York City. Her passion for art transcends into a unique initiative, The Art at the Table, where she combines culinary experiences with artistic expression.

Balancing her professional life, Kesía is also a devoted homeschooling mother of two, illustrating her remarkable ability to juggle multiple responsibilities with grace and efficiency. Her journey reflects professional success and a deep commitment to family and personal growth.

Recommended Professional Contacts

In navigating the art world's legal landscape, having access to knowledgeable and trustworthy professionals can make a significant difference. Below are two individuals whose expertise has been invaluable to me and may serve you well:

Leyla Ramos - Contract Review Attorney: Leyla brings a keen eye for detail and a deep understanding of the nuances in art contracts. Her guidance can help you navigate complex agreements, protecting your rights and interests.

    Email: lramosesq@gmail.com

    Phone: 786.209.5222

Andrew Gerber - Copyright Infringement Specialist: Specializing in copyright law, Andrew has a proven track record of successfully defending artists' rights. Andrew's expertise is indispensable for copyright infringement concerns or litigation needs.

    Email: andrew@kgfirm.com

    Phone: 212.882.1320

    Website: https://www.kgfirm.com/

These professionals have been instrumental in my journey, and I recommend them to any artist seeking legal advice or services.

APPENDICES

Example Art Disclosure Statement

Artist Name: [Artist's Full Name]

Title of Artwork: [Title of the Work]

Date of Creation: [Date]

Medium and Materials Used: [Description of materials and medium used]

1. Description of the Artwork

- Provide a brief artwork description, including style, dimensions, and unique features.

2. Condition of the Artwork:

- State the artwork's current condition and disclose any imperfections, damages, or restoration work that has been done.

3. Provenance and History:

- Detail the history of the artwork, including previous owners, if applicable, exhibitions where the artwork was displayed, and any awards or recognitions received.

4. Authentication:

- Verify the authenticity of the artwork. Include details of any certificates of authenticity or appraisals that accompany the piece.

5. Care and Maintenance Instructions:

- Provide specific instructions on how to care for and maintain the artwork, including handling, cleaning, and storage recommendations.

6. Additional Information:

- Disclose any other relevant information, such as the artwork's edition number (for prints or limited editions), whether the artwork is part of a series, or any other significant aspects related to the artwork.

7. Artist's Statement:

- [Optional] Include a brief statement about the artwork's inspiration, concept, or context, providing deeper insight into the work.

8. Acknowledgment of Receipt:

- I, [Buyer's Name], acknowledge receipt of this disclosure and understand the details described above regarding the artwork titled [Title of the Artwork].

Buyer

    Signature: _____

    Date: _____

Artist

    Signature: _____

    Date: _____

Sample Collaboration Agreement Template for Artists

Title: Collaboration Agreement between [Artist 1] and [Artist 2]

Date: [Insert Date]

Parties Involved:

1. [Artist 1 Name], [Contact Information]
2. [Artist 2 Name], [Contact Information]

Project Description:

- Briefly describe the collaborative project, including the artistic concept, medium, and intended outcome or final product.

Roles and Responsibilities:

- [Artist 1's Responsibilities]: Outline specific tasks and contributions.
- [Artist 2's Responsibilities]: Outline specific tasks and contributions.

Financial Terms:

- **Budget:** Detail the project's budget, including contributions from each artist.
- **Profit Sharing:** Specify how profits or revenues will be divided between the artists.
- **Expenses:** Outline how costs will be shared and managed.

Intellectual Property:

- **Ownership:** Define how the intellectual property rights of the collaborative work will be owned and shared.
- **Usage Rights:** Specify how artists can use the collaborative work for their portfolios, exhibitions, or sales.

Duration and Termination:

- **Project Timeline:** Specify the start and end dates of the collaboration.
- **Termination Clauses:** Conditions under which the collaboration agreement can be terminated.

Dispute Resolution:

- Define the process for resolving any disputes that may arise during the collaboration.

Miscellaneous:

- **Confidentiality:** Any terms regarding the confidentiality of the project details.
- **Amendments:** The process for making any changes to this agreement.

Signatures:

- Both parties should thoroughly review and sign the agreement, indicating their understanding and acceptance of all terms.

Artist 1

  Signature: _____

  Date: _____

Artist 2

  Signature: _____

  Date: _____

Rights Protection Checklist

Objective: To assist artists in safeguarding their rights in every artistic engagement, whether it involves creating, displaying, or selling their work.

Rights Protection Checklist:

1. Copyright Registration:

- Ensure that your work is registered for copyright protection, if applicable.
- Keep a record of registration details for future reference.

2. Review and Understand Contracts:

- Carefully read and understand all contracts before signing.
- Look for clauses related to copyright transfer, licensing, and royalties.

3. Negotiate Favorable Terms:

- Feel free to negotiate contract terms that better protect your rights.
- Consider consulting a legal professional for significant contracts.

4. Document Your Creative Process:

- Keep a record of your creative process, including sketches, drafts, and notes.
- This documentation can be crucial in proving originality and ownership.

5. Moral Rights Assertion:

- Be aware of your moral rights, including the right to attribution, and protect your work from distortion.
- Assert these rights in contracts where appropriate.

6. Licensing Agreements:

- If licensing your work, ensure the terms are clear about usage, duration, and compensation.
- Retain copies of all licensing agreements.

7. Digital Art Considerations:

- Consider measures like watermarking and digital rights management (DRM) tools for digital artwork.
- Be clear about digital distribution rights in any agreements.

8. Handling Infringement:

- Have a plan for addressing potential copyright infringement, including sending cease-and-desist letters or seeking legal counsel.
- Document all instances of infringement.

9. Public Display and Performance Rights:

- If your work is publicly displayed or performed, ensure the terms respect your rights and offer appropriate compensation.

10. Stay Informed:

- Keep up to date with changes in copyright law and legal rights relevant to artists.
- Join artist advocacy groups or subscribe to legal newsletters in the arts sector.

Contract Review Checklist for Artists

Purpose: This checklist is designed to help artists thoroughly review and understand the terms of any contract they are considering, ensuring their interests are protected.

1. Identify the Parties Involved:

- Ensure all parties' names and contact information (including yours) are correct.

2. Clarify the Scope of Work:

- What exactly are you being hired to do?
- Are the expectations and deliverables clearly defined?

3. Check the Timeline:

- Are the start and completion dates realistic?
- Is there an explicit schedule for milestones or deadlines?

4. Review Financial Terms:

- What is the total compensation and payment schedule?
- Are expenses and materials costs covered separately?

5. Understand Copyright and Intellectual Property Rights:

- Who retains the copyright?
- Are there any rights being licensed or transferred?

6. Examine Licensing Terms (if applicable):

- What rights are you granting, and for how long?
- Are there any geographical limitations?

7. Look at Termination Clauses:

- Under what conditions can either party terminate the contract?
- What are the consequences of early termination?

8. Review Confidentiality Requirements (if any):

- Are there any non-disclosure terms?
- How long does the confidentiality requirement last?

9. Consider Non-Compete and Exclusivity Clauses:

- Are you restricted from working with others or on similar projects?
- How long do these restrictions last?

10. Assess Liability and Indemnification:

- Are there clauses that could hold you liable for specific issues?
- What legal protections are in place for you?

11. Check Dispute Resolution Terms:

- How are disputes to be resolved?
- Is there an arbitration or mediation clause?

12. Confirm Jurisdiction and Governing Law:

- Under which state or country's laws will the contract be governed?

13. Other Clauses and Special Considerations:

- Are there any unusual or unclear clauses?
- Do you understand all the terms and conditions?

14. Seek Professional Advice:

- Consider having a lawyer or legal expert review the contract, especially for high-value or complex agreements.

15. Final Review and Negotiation:

- Are there any terms you wish to negotiate or clarify?
- Ensure you are comfortable with all aspects of the contract before signing.

Legal Toolkit for Artists

1. Contract Templates:

- **Art Commission Contract Template:** https://www.
  pandadoc.com/art-commission-agreement/ https://www.
  hellobonsai.com/contract-template/artist
- **Licensing Agreement Template:** https://www.wonder.
  legal/modele/licensing-agreement
- **Collaboration Agreement Template:** https://www.
  wonder.legal/modele/collaboration-agreement

2. Intellectual Property Resources:

- **Copyright Registration Guide:** https://www.
  copyright.gov/
- **Trademark Application Process for Artists:** https://www.
  uspto.gov/
- **Online Intellectual Property Rights Resources:** https://
  www.stopfakes.gov/welcome

3. Legal Services and Assistance:

- **Directory of Legal Services Specializing in Art Law:**
  https://itsartlaw.org/law-firms/
- **List of Pro Bono Legal Services for Artists:** https://vlany.
  org/national-directory-of-volunteer-lawyers-for-the-arts/
- **Contacts for Artist Advocacy Groups:** https://
  artistcommunities.org/cultural-advocacy-group

4. Digital Art Resources:

- **Guide to Digital Rights Management (DRM) for Artists:** https://www.digitalguardian.com/blog/what-digital-rights-management
- **NFT Platforms Overview and Best Practices:** https://101blockchains.com/nft-development-guide/
- **Online Art Sales and Copyright Guide:** https://www.gerbenlaw.com/blog/nfts-and-trademarks-gerbens-complete-guide/

5. Dispute Resolution Tools:

- **Template for Cease-and-Desist Letters:** https://eforms.com/cease-and-desist/
- **Steps for Handling Art-Related Legal Disputes:** https://itsartlaw.org/2019/03/29/cheers-a-new-court-for-resolving-art-disputes/

6. Professional Development Resources:

- **Workshops and Seminars on Art Law:** https://itsartlaw.org/all-events/
- **Educational Materials on Negotiation and Contract Management:** https://www.pon.harvard.edu/ https://ocw.mit.edu/
- **Online Courses on Intellectual Property Rights for Artists:** https://www.coursera.org/courses?query=intellectual%20property https://www.edx.org/learn/intellectual-property https://www.wipo.int/academy/en/courses/distance_learning/

7. Documentation and Record-Keeping Tools:

- **Artwork Documentation and Cataloging Tips:** https://www.artworkarchive.com/blog/how-to-catalog-your-fine-art-collection
- **Templates for Inventory Management and Sales Tracking:** https://www.jotform.com/table-templates/art-inventory-template

8. Online Platform Guidelines:

- **Legal Considerations for Selling Art on Online Platforms:** https://blog.daisie.com/online-art-sale-a-guide-to-legal-hurdles/
- **Social Media and Copyright Best Practices for Artists:** https://tingen.law/2021/best-practices-to-help-you-protect-your-copyright/50542/
- **Tips for Protecting Artwork in Digital Spaces:** https://emptyeasel.com/2017/07/31/8-ways-to-protect-your-artwork-images-from-being-copied-online/

9. Legal Updates and News:

- **Subscription Links to Legal Newsletters Focused on the Art World:** https://artbizsuccess.com/ https://theabundantartist.com/ https://www.artsyshark.com/2015/09/03/organize-your-art-business/
- **Blogs and Websites for Staying Updated on Art Law Developments:** https://lawlibguides.luc.edu/c.php?g=610827&p=4239299

Glossary of Legal Terms for Artists

1. Copyright:

Simple Explanation: A legal right that protects your original art. It stops others from using, copying, or selling your work without your permission.

2. Licensing:

Simple Explanation: When you give someone permission to use your artwork under certain conditions, for a fee, or in specific ways.

3. Intellectual Property:

Simple Explanation: The legal term for creations of your mind, like art, designs, and symbols. It includes things you can't touch but have value because they're original.

4. Work-for-Hire:

Simple Explanation: When you create art as part of a job or commission, and the person who hired you owns the work, not you.

5. Indemnification:

Simple Explanation: A promise in a contract where one party agrees to protect the other from any losses or damages related to the contract.

6. Jurisdiction:

Simple Explanation: The area or scope where specific laws apply and where a legal body can make decisions.

7. Royalties:

Simple Explanation: Money you get paid for allowing others to use or sell your art, usually a percentage of their sales or profits.

8. Confidentiality Agreement:

Simple Explanation: A promise to keep certain information secret. It's often part of contracts to protect sensitive information about a project or artwork.

9. Assignment Clause:

Simple Explanation: Part of a contract that lets one party transfer their rights and duties to someone else.

10. Termination Clause:

Simple Explanation: This is a part of a contract that explains how and when the contract can end before its original completion date.

11. Force Majeure:

Simple Explanation: A clause in contracts that frees both parties from obligation if an uncontrollable event (like a natural disaster) prevents them from fulfilling the contract.

12. Non-Compete Clause:

Simple Explanation: A part of a contract that stops you from working on similar projects with competitors for a particular time and in a specific area.

13. Mediation:

Simple Explanation: A way to solve disputes where a neutral third person helps the conflicting parties reach an agreement.

14. Arbitration:

Simple Explanation: Like a private court case, where a neutral third person hears both sides and makes a usually binding decision.

15. Moral Rights:

Simple Explanation: Rights that protect your work's personal and reputational value, like the right to be credited as the artist.

16. NFT (Non-Fungible Token):

Simple Explanation: A unique digital certificate stored on a blockchain shows ownership of a digital asset, like digital art.

17. DMCA (Digital Millennium Copyright Act):

Simple Explanation: A law that helps protect digital content from being copied and shared without permission.

18. VARA (Visual Artists Rights Act):

Simple Explanation: A law that protects artists' moral rights, like preventing unwanted changes to their work, even if they no longer own it.